Selecting
WINES FOR FOOD
Simply

Richard "Ric" Dunseth

Library of Congress Catalog Card No. 96-061156

ISBN 1-56550-064-4

Printed in the United States of America

Cover art: Michele Collier
Cover graphics and design: Robert Brekke

Simply Books
P.O. Box 371
Calistoga, CA 94515
707-942-0562
Fax: 707-942-6774

Acknowledgment

To my wife, Linda

…who wouldn't cook and thus has made me the ardent cook that I have become…who stocked my wine cellar but wouldn't let me touch it. "Let it age!"

To write a book on selecting wine for food, one must taste the wine and foods, thus the wine cellar was opened. Tough job, but someone needed to do it. Why not me?

Special thanks to Robert Brekke who has led, pushed, cajoled, and taught me the publishing process.

Thanks also to the publisher, Ken Sackett, for taking a chance.

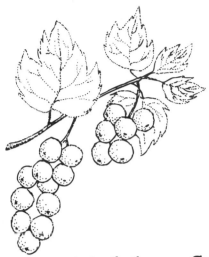

Table of Contents

Introduction

This book takes the mystique out of wine and food pairing.

If you've ever wondered which wine to serve with Thanksgiving dinner, a special dessert, or even popcorn, the tried-and-true answers lie within. Whether you're a novice or an experienced connoisseur, you'll find easy-to-understand answers to common questions about selecting wine for food.

As you read through these pages you will find many wine and food choices, but don't be overwhelmed! I've simplified this wine and food pairing process into three sections:

- A wine section; from the respective wine page, select a food.
- A food section; from the respective food page, select a wine.
- A menu section; includes wine choices and selected recipes.

Also for your use, the pages include a **"notes"** section. If you're pleased with the tastes–you can note it; if not–you can note that also. Use these note sections at your discretion. Add your own favorites and maybe "Auntie Kathy's," or just simply enjoy the adventure.

Use this book while planning your meal and writing your grocery list. This can lighten the chore and portend the wonderful tastes to come. Refer to it in the kitchen while you are cooking (even if the pages get sticky). Use it. Abuse it. That's why you bought it! Enjoy!

Wine Tasting

Wine tasting is not only fun, but can also be informative. Pour about an ounce of wine in a wine glass. Holding the glass by the stem, look at the color and clarity. Swirl to aerate and smell (don't be afraid to put your nose in the glass). Now taste.

Color can vary, but the wine must be clear (not hazy), although a small amount of sediment is acceptable. Different white wine types can have many shades of yellow, from pale straw to dark gold, from hints of green to shades of brown. Red wine types can vary from light red to a crimson purple, aging to a brownish tint.

Swirling the wine ("letting it open") releases smells ("aromas") that you may not have been aware were even present (the "nose"). These aromas can include: oak (vanilla), mixed fruit or floral, even specific scents such as violets, pears, melons, or berries. These same scents release little bursts of flavor in the wine that usually linger on your palate long after you've swallowed the wine (the "finish").

This enjoyable experience is only part of the excitement. The other is tasting the wine with food and discovering how each can complement the other.

Why you may want to decant your wine:
    Sediment - any sediment - will settle to the bottom
      of the decanter
    Aeration - lets the wine "breathe"- increases aroma
    Temperature - warms it if it is too cold
    Theatrics - show

"Wine tasting, in the classic phrase, is a diverting pastime for young and old, for ladies as well as men. It is not so intellectual as chamber music...nor will anyone entangle you with problems that need an intimate understanding of Einstein. It is, in fact, the ideal pursuit with which to while away those hours between eleven in the morning and four in the afternoon."

Anonymous

Bottle Sizes

United States adaptations and estimated servings

Terminology	Capacity	Bottle	Servings
Split	187ML	1/4	1
Half bottle	375ML	1/2	2
Full bottle	750ML	1	4
Magnum	1.5L	2	8
Double magnum	3L	4	16
Jeroboam	3L	4	16
Rehoboam	4.5L	6	24
Imperial	6L	8	32
Methusalem	6L	8	32
Salmanazar	9L	12	48
Balthazar	12L	16	64
Nebuchadnezzar	12-16L	16-20	64-85
Sovereign	50L	67	278

BOTTLE = standard size wine or champagne bottle:
750 ML or 4/5 qt.

Key

Use this key when you need to refresh yourself with wine terminology, or to assist you in making a wine selection. The wine descriptions given are general.

Terminology

Body	Fullness; richness
Finish	Length of time flavors linger
Fruity	Aroma and taste; can be dry or slightly sweet
Nose	Aroma, bouquet

Wines

Dry	Not sweet
Semi-dry	Hint of sweetness or fruitiness
Semi-sweet	Little sweetness
Dessert Wines	Sweet
Late Harvest	Very sweet

Sparkling Wines / Champagnes*

*These names are used synonymously in the U.S.A. Champagnes are stylistic (vary slightly from winery to winery).

Blanc de Blancs	Hints of fruit; dry
Blanc de Noirs	Fruity, hint of sweetness (pink in color)
Brut	Rich; dry
Extra Dry	Semi-sweet

Serving Temperatures

Champagnes	50° (refrigerator temperature)
Sparkling Wines	50°
White Wines	45 - 55°
Rosé Wines	45 - 50°
Red Wines	55 - 65° (cool cellar temperature)
White Dessert Wines	40 - 45°
Red Dessert Wines	55 - 65°

WINES

**Champagne and
Sparkling Wines
White Wines
Rosé Wines
Red Wines
Dessert Wines**

Select The Wine, Choose The Food

*The wine aromas often will carry over, adding to the flavor.
Food-friendly wines are high in acid, low in alcohol.
Big foods require big wines high in alcohol.*

By wine we are generous made,
It furnishes fancy with wings;
Without it we would ne' er had
Philosophers, poets or kings.

The Rubaiyat of Omar Khayyam

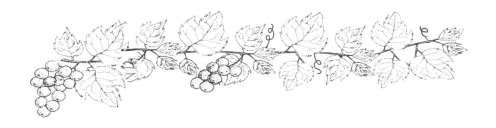

Champagne and Sparkling Wines

Blanc de Blancs
Blanc de Noirs
Brut
Extra Dry

These wines were traditionally served with
caviar, paté de foie gras, and smoked salmon. Now, they
are so much more than "special occasion" wines
and are enjoyed with many food choices.

And we meet, with champagne . . . at last.

Lady Mary Wortley Montagu (1689-1762)
The Lover 1748

Blanc de Blancs

Blanc de Blanc translates to white of white meaning white champagne made from green (white) grapes; hints of fruit; delicate; semi-dry.

—— *Notes* ——

CHEESES
Mild
Soft - Creamy

ETHNIC FOODS
French
Oriental

FRUITS
Fleshy
Melons
Berries

MEATS
Pork
Veal

POULTRY
Light

SALADS
Vinegar dressings
Creamy dressings

SAUCES
Creamy

SAUSAGES
Light

SEAFOOD
Fish
Shellfish

SOUPS
Creamy
Light

VEGETABLES
Leafy
Root

Blanc de Noirs

Blanc de Noirs translates to white of black meaning white champagne made from red (black) grapes; fruity; hints of sweetness; pink.

CHEESES
- Mild
- Pungent
- Soft - Creamy

DESSERTS
- Chocolate
- Cream
- Fruit

ETHNIC FOODS
- Cajun
- French
- Oriental

FRUITS
- Fleshy
- Melons
- Berries

MEATS
- Cured
- Lamb
- Pork
- Veal

POULTRY
- Light

SALADS
- Vinegar dressing

SAUCES
- Creamy

SAUSAGES
- Light

SEAFOOD
- Shellfish

SOUPS
- Creamy

VEGETABLES
- Root

—— *Notes* ——

Brut

Traditional champagne, usually a blend of Chardonnay (green grapes) and Pinot Noir (red grapes); baked bread aroma; rich flavor; dry.

——— Notes ———

CHEESES
Hard - Dry
Mild

ETHNIC FOODS
French

FRUITS
Fleshy
Melons
Berries

MEATS
Cured
Lamb
Pork
Veal

POULTRY
Dark
Light

SALADS
Vinegar dressings
Creamy dressings

SAUCES
Creamy
Gravies

SAUSAGES
Light

SEAFOOD
Fish
Shellfish

SOUPS
Creamy
Light

VEGETABLES
Leafy
Root

Extra Dry

Usually made from a brut blend with additional sugar; rich flavor, semi-sweet, gold in color.

CHEESES
Mild
Pungent
Soft - Creamy

DESSERTS
Chocolate
Cream
Fruit

ETHNIC FOODS
Cajun
Oriental

FRUITS
Fleshy
Melons
Berries

MEAT
Cured
Pork
Veal

POULTRY
Light

SALADS
Vinegar dressings

SAUCES
Creamy

SAUSAGES
Light

SEAFOOD
Fish
Shellfish

SOUPS
Creamy
Light

VEGETABLES
Root

—— *Notes* ——

White Wines

Chablis
Chardonnay
Chenin Blanc
Gerwürztraminer
Riesling
Sake
Sauvignon Blanc/Fumé Blanc

Fill ev'ry glass, for wine inspires us...

John Gay (1688-1732)

Chablis

American blended white table wines; grape and fruit aromas
and flavors, varies in sweetness, lighter style;
good all-purpose match.

―― *Notes* ――

CHEESES
   Hard - Dry
   Mild
   Soft - Creamy

FRUITS
   Fleshy
   Melons
   Berries

ETHNIC FOODS
   Cajun
   Oriental

MEATS
   Pork
   Veal

POULTRY
   Light

SALADS
   Vinegar dressings

SAUCES
   Creamy

SAUSAGES
   Light

SEAFOOD
   Fish
   Shellfish

SOUPS
   Creamy
   Light

VEGETABLES
   Leafy

Chardonnay

The dominating fruit character is an appealing green apple flavor, the style can be buttery-oak or fruity in aroma and flavor; dry.

CHEESES
Hard - Dry
Mild
Pungent
Soft - Creamy

DESSERTS
Chocolate
Cream
Fruit

ETHNIC FOODS
French
Oriental

FRUITS
Fleshy
Melons
Berries

MEATS
Lamb
Pork
Veal

POULTRY
Light

SALADS
Creamy dressings

SAUCES
Creamy

SAUSAGES
Light

SOUP
Creamy
Light

SEAFOOD
Fish
Shellfish

VEGETABLES
Leafy
Root

—— *Notes* ——

Chenin Blanc

A mellow, pleasant wine; floral and fruity aromas and flavors; slightly sweet.

—— *Notes* ——

CHEESES
Hard - Dry
Mild
Pungent
Soft - Creamy

DESSERTS
Chocolate
Cream
Fruit

ETHNIC FOODS
Cajun
Oriental

FRUITS
Fleshy
Melons
Berries

MEATS
Cured
Pork
Veal

POULTRY
Light

SALADS
Vinegar dressings
Creamy dressings

SAUCES
Creamy

SAUSAGES
Light

SEAFOOD
Fish
Shellfish

SOUPS
Creamy
Light

VEGETABLES
Leafy

Gerwürztraminer

Lively wine with spicy character; hints of cinnamon, ginger, nutmeg, and apple; semi-dry.

CHEESES
Pungent
Soft - Creamy

DESSERTS
Chocolate
Cream
Fruit

ETHNIC FOODS
Cajun
Oriental

FRUITS
Fleshy
Melons
Berries

MEATS
Cured
Pork
Veal

POULTRY
Light

SALADS
Vinegar dressings
Creamy dressings

SAUCES
Creamy
Gravies

SAUSAGES
Light

SEAFOOD
Fish
Shellfish

—— *Notes* ——

Riesling

Layer of floral and fruit aromas and flavors; dry or sweet.
This book pairs with sweet only.

—— *Notes* ——

CHEESES
Pungent
Soft - Creamy

DESSERTS
Chocolate
Cream
Fruit

ETHNIC FOODS
Cajun
Oriental

FRUITS
Fleshy
Melons
Berries

MEATS
Cured
Pork
Veal

SALADS
Vinegar dressings
Creamy dressings

SAUCES
Creamy
Gravies

SAUSAGES
Light

SEAFOOD
Fish
Shellfish

Sake

"Wine" fermented from rice; served warm or cold, usually with Oriental food; also used for wine daiquiris, margaritas.

ORIENTAL FOODS
Sashimi
Sukiyaki
Sushi
Tempura
Teriyaki

VEGETABLES
Leafy
Root

—— *Notes* ——

Sauvignon Blanc/Fume Blanc

This is the same wine given two different names. Very fragrant, can be grassy or fruity in aroma, fruity taste, green olive and bell pepper flavors; dry.

—— *Notes* ——

CHEESES
Hard - Dry
Pungent
Soft - Creamy

ETHNIC FOODS
Cajun
French
Oriental

FRUITS
Berries

MEATS
Cured
Lamb
Pork
Veal

POULTRY
Light

SALADS
Vinegar dressings
Creamy dressings

SAUCES
Creamy

SAUSAGES
Light

SEAFOOD
Fish
Shellfish

SOUPS
Light
Creamy

VEGETABLES
Leafy
Root

Rosé Wines

Blush Wines
Vin Rosé
White Zinfandel

'Tis spring in a glass....

Ric Dunseth

Blush Wines

Generally made from Cabernet grapes; raspberry aroma, currant, spicy flavor; light body, semi-dry.

—— *Notes* ——

CHEESES
Hard - Dry
Mild
Pungent

DESSERTS
Chocolate
Cream
Fruit

ETHNIC FOODS
Cajun

FRUITS
Fleshy
Melons
Berries

MEATS
Barbecued
Beef
Cured
Lamb
Pork
Veal

POULTRY
Dark

SALADS
Vinegar dressing
Creamy dressing

SAUCES
Tomato

SAUSAGES
Dark

SEAFOOD
Shellfish

SOUPS
Hearty

VEGETABLES
Root

21

Vin Rosé

A blend of various red grapes; usually fruity and berry-like flavors; light body, semi-sweet.

CANDY

CHEESES
Mild
Soft - Creamy

DESSERTS
Chocolate
Cream
Fruit

ETHNIC FOODS
Cajun
Oriental

FRUITS
Fleshy
Melons
Berries

MEATS
Pork
Veal

POULTRY
Light

SALADS
Vinegar dressing
Creamy dressing

SAUCES
Creamy

SAUSAGES
Light

SEAFOOD
Fish
Shellfish

SOUPS
Creamy

VEGETABLES
Leafy

—— *Notes* ——

White Zinfandel

Made from Zinfandel grapes, but fermented without their red skins; spicy, floral, and fruity in aroma and taste; semi-sweet.

—— *Notes* ——

CANDY

CHEESES
Mild
Soft - Creamy

DESSERTS
Chocolate
Cream
Fruit

ETHNIC FOODS
Cajun
Oriental

FRUITS
Fleshy
Melons
Berries

MEATS
Barbecued
Cured
Pork
Veal

POULTRY
Light

SALADS
Vinegar dressing
Creamy dressing

SAUCES
Creamy

SAUSAGES
Light
Dark

SEAFOOD
Fish
Shellfish

SOUPS
Creamy

VEGETABLES
Leafy

23

Red Wines

Barbera
Burgundy
Cabernet Sauvignon
Gamay Beaujolais
Merlot
Petite Sirah
Pinot Noir
Zinfandel

To happy convents, bosom'd deep in vines,
where slumber abbots, purple as their vines.

Alexander Pope The Dunciad. Book iv

Barbera

Clove, cinnamon, black cherry, or alfalfa aromas with light pepper and pleasant tartness, fruit flavors, full-bodied; very dry.

—— *Notes* ——

CHEESE
Hard - Dry
Pungent

ETHNIC FOODS
Italian

MEATS
Barbecued
Beef
Cured
Lamb
Rabbit
Ribs
Smoked
Wild game

POULTRY
Dark

SAUCES
Gravies
Tomato

SAUSAGES
Dark

SOUPS
Hearty

Burgundy

American blended red table wines; grapey and fruity aroma and flavor, generally lighter style; good all-purpose match.

CHEESES
Hard - Dry
Mild
Soft - Creamy

ETHNIC FOODS
Cajun
Italian

MEATS
Beef
Cured
Ribs
Veal

POULTRY
Dark

SAUCES
Gravies
Tomato

SAUSAGES
Light
Dark

SOUPS
Hearty

VEGETABLES
Root

—— *Notes* ——

Cabernet Sauvignon

Fruit jam, plum, mint, tea, green pepper, black pepper and berry-like aromas and flavors or can have a chocolate and honey bouquet and flavors, big body; dry.

—— *Notes* ——

CHEESES
Pungent

DESSERTS
Chocolate

ETHNIC FOODS
French
Italian

MEATS
Barbecued
Beef
Lamb
Rabbit
Smoked
Wild game

POULTRY
Dark

SAUCES
Gravies
Tomato

SAUSAGES
Light
Dark

SOUPS
Hearty

Gamay Beaujolais

Light cherry and grape aromas, cranberry, pomegranate and
watermelon flavors, medium body; semi-dry.

CHEESES
Hard - Dry
Mild
Soft - Creamy

DESSERTS
Chocolate
Cream
Fruit

ETHNIC FOODS
French

FRUITS
Fleshy
Melons
Berries

MEATS
Cured
Lamb
Pork
Veal

POULTRY
Dark

SALADS
Vinegar dressings
Creamy dressings

SAUSAGES
Dark

SEAFOOD
Shellfish

SOUPS
Hearty

VEGETABLES
Root

—— *Notes* ——

Merlot

Mint, tea, or fruit aroma; plum, cherry, herb flavors, velvety soft with a smoky bouquet, full body; dry.

—— *Notes* ——

CHEESES
Hard - Dry
Soft - Creamy

DESSERTS
Chocolate

ETHNIC FOODS
French
Italian

MEATS
Barbecued
Beef
Cured
Lamb
Pork
Rabbit
Ribs
Wild game

POULTRY
Dark

SAUCES
Gravies
Tomato

SAUSAGES
Dark

SOUPS
Hearty

Petite Sirah

The name "Petite" is very misleading. This is a full-bodied wine with blackberry, pepper and plum aromas and flavors; dry.

CHEESES
Hard - Dry
Pungent

DESSERTS
Chocolate

ETHNIC FOODS
Cajun
Italian

MEATS
Barbecued
Beef
Cured
Lamb
Smoked
Wild game

POULTRY
Dark

SAUCES
Gravies
Tomato

SAUSAGES
Dark

SOUPS
Hearty

—— *Notes* ——

Pinot Noir

Floral and strawberry aromas, rich in cherry, licorice or cigar-box flavor, medium body; semi-dry.

—— *Notes* ——

CHEESES
Hard - Dry
Mild
Soft - Creamy

DESSERTS
Chocolate
Cream
Fruit

ETHNIC FOODS
Cajun
French

FRUITS
Fleshy
Melons
Berries

MEATS
Beef
Cured
Lamb
Pork
Rabbit
Veal

POULTRY
Dark
Light

SAUCES
Gravies

SAUSAGES
Dark
Light

SEAFOOD
Shellfish

SOUPS
Hearty

Zinfandel

Raspberry and currant aroma adds to an earthy bouquet and spicy flavor, medium to full body; dry.

CHEESES
Hard - Dry
Mild
Pungent
Soft - Creamy

DESSERTS
Chocolate

ETHNIC FOODS
Cajun
Italian

MEATS
Barbecued
Beef
Cured
Lamb
Rabbit
Wild game

POULTRY
Dark

SALADS
Creamy dressings

SAUCES
Gravy
Tomato

SAUSAGES
Dark

SOUPS
Hearty

VEGETABLES
Root

—— *Notes* ——

Dessert Wines

Muscato
Port
Sherry

A fine repast, and now, a glass.

Ric Dunseth

Muscato

Also known as muscat in the United States; ripe melons, ripe fruit, honeysuckle, aromas and flavors; sweet.

—— *notes* ——

CANDY

CHEESES
   Mild
   Pungent
   Soft - Creamy

DESSERTS
   Cream
   Fruit

ETHNIC FOODS
   Oriental

FRUITS
   Berries
   Fleshy
   Melons

SOUPS
   Creamy

Port

Raisin and spice aromas, also flavored by the cask in which it is aged; full body; usually very sweet.

CHEESES
Hard - Dry
Mild
Pungent
Sharp

DESSERTS
Chocolate
Cream
Fruit

FRUITS
Berries
Fleshy

MEATS
Cured
Smoked

SAUCES
Creamy

SEAFOOD
Shellfish

SOUPS
Hearty

—— *Notes* ——

Sherry

Blended wines and fortified with brandy; butterscotch aroma, nutty, woody flavor; varies in sweetness.

—— *Notes* ——

CHEESES
Hard - Dry
Mild
Pungent
Sharp
Soft - Creamy

DESSERTS
Cream
Fruit

ETHNIC FOODS
French
Oriental

MEATS
Cured
Smoked

SAUCES
Creamy

SEAFOOD
Shellfish

SOUPS
Creamy

FOODS

Cheeses
Desserts
Ethnic Foods
Fruits
Meats
Poultry
Salads
Sauces
Sausages
Seafood
Soups
Vegetables

Choose The Food, Select The Wine

If the specific item you wish to pair is not listed, i.e.
shrimp in a cream sauce, simply compare the seafood page
with the sauce page and choose the common wine.

Go, eat thy bread with enjoyment,
and drink thy wine with a merry heart,...

The Bible. Ecclesiastes 9:7

Hint: When in doubt, the food must be less sweet than the wine with which it is served, and the heavier the food, the heartier the wine.

Cheeses

Hard–Dry
Mild
Pungent
Soft–Creamy

Because cheeses vary considerably in flavor, dryness, and texture, selecting the "perfect" wine to serve with them is more challenging but also more fun than just picking a red wine to serve with spaghetti. This list will get you started. As you progress, try different wines to enjoy the regional differences associated with cheese- making (cow/goat milk, curing/aging, etc.).

Hard-Dry

Parmesan, Romano, Asiago

—— *Notes* ——

CHAMPAGNE
Brut *7*

WHITE WINE
Chablis *11*
Chardonnay *12*
Chenin Blanc *13*
Sauvignon Blanc *17*

ROSÉ WINE
Blush *21*

RED WINE
Barbera *27*
Burgundy *28*
Gamay Beaujolais *30*
Merlot *31*
Petite Sirah *32*
Pinot Noir *33*
Zinfandel *34*

DESSERT WINE
Port *38*
Sherry *39*

Cheeses

Mild

Monterey Jack, Havarti, Mild Cheddar

CHAMPAGNE
Blanc de Blancs *5*
Blanc de Noirs *6*
Brut *7*
Extra Dry *8*

WHITE WINE
Chablis *11*
Chardonnay *12*
Chenin Blanc *13*

ROSÉ WINE
Blush *21*
Vin Rosé *22*
White Zinfandel *23*

RED WINE
Burgundy *28*
Gamay Beaujolais *30*
Pinot Noir *33*
Zinfandel *34*

DESSERT WINE
Muscato *37*
Port *38*
Sherry *39*

—— *Notes* ——

Pungent

Limburger, Roquefort, Blue

—— *Notes* ——

CHAMPAGNE
Blanc de Noirs *6*
Extra Dry *8*

WHITE WINE
Chardonnay *12*
Chenin Blanc *13*
Gerwürztraminer *14*
Riesling *15*
Sauvignon Blanc *17*

ROSÉ WINE
Blush *21*

RED WINE
Barbera *27*
Cabernet Sauvignon *29*
Petite Sirah *32*
Zinfandel *34*

DESSERT WINE
Port *38*
Sherry *39*

Cheeses

Soft ~ Creamy

Brie, Farmers, Gourmandise

────── *Notes* ──────

CHAMPAGNE
Blanc de Blancs *5*
Blanc de Noirs *6*
Extra Dry *8*

WHITE WINE
Chablis *11*
Chardonnay *12*
Chenin Blanc *13*
Gerwürztraminer *14*
Riesling *15*
Sauvignon Blanc *17*

ROSÉ WINE
Vin Rosé *22*
White Zinfandel *23*

RED WINE
Burgundy *28*
Gamay Beaujolais *30*
Merlot *31*
Pinot Noir *33*
Zinfandel *34*

DESSERT WINE
Muscato *37*
Sherry *39*

Desserts

Chocolate
Cream
Fruit

This section is for rich desserts, including all chocolates, cakes, custard, and fruit desserts. In most cases, I did not include heavy red wines with the dessert, but there are exceptions, such as a Cabernet Sauvignon with chocolate mousse. This section probably shouldn't be used by the diet conscious (unless you skip the dessert and drink the wine).

Chocolate

Candy, Decadent Cakes and Mousses

—— *Notes* ——

CHAMPAGNE
    Blanc de Noirs *6*
    Extra Dry *8*

WHITE WINE
    Chardonnay *12*
    Chenin Blanc *13*
    Gerwürztraminer *14*
    Riesling *15*

ROSÉ WINE
    Blush *21*
    Vin Rosé *22*
    White Zinfandel *23*

RED WINE
    Cabernet Sauvignon *29*
    Gamay Beaujolais *30*
    Merlot *31*
    Petite Sirah *32*
    Pinot Noir *33*
    Zinfandel *34*

DESSERT WINE
    Port *38*

Desserts

Cream Desserts

Cakes, Custards, Mousses, and Puddings

CHAMPAGNE
Blanc de Noirs *6*
Extra Dry *8*

WHITE WINE
Chardonnay *12*
Chenin Blanc *13*
Gerwürztraminer *14*
Riesling *15*

ROSÉ WINE
Blush *21*
Vin Rosé *22*
White Zinfandel *23*

RED WINE
Gamay Beaujolais *30*
Pinot Noir *33*

DESSERT WINE
Muscato *37*
Port *38*
Sherry *39*

—— *Notes* ——

Fruit

Pies and Tarts

— Notes —

CHAMPAGNE
Blanc de Noirs *6*
Extra Dry *8*

WHITE WINE
Chardonnay *12*
Chenin Blanc *13*
Gerwürztraminer *14*
Riesling *15*

ROSÉ WINE
Blush *21*
Vin Rosé *22*
White Zinfandel *23*

RED WINE
Gamay Beaujolais *30*
Pinot Noir *33*

DESSERT WINE
Muscato *37*
Port *38*
Sherry *39*

Desserts

Ethnic Foods

Cajun
French
Italian
Oriental

These pairings are very general, as the categories are broad and the dishes will vary depending on locale. Experiment! The worst case is that your palate may make a new discovery.

Cajun

If it has a burned roux, blackened exterior, or is Louisiana hot—it must be Cajun.

—— *Notes* ——

CHAMPAGNE
> Blanc de Noirs *6*
> Extra Dry *8*

WHITE WINE
> Chablis *11*
> Chenin Blanc *13*
> Gerwürztraminer *14*
> Riesling *15*
> Sauvignon Blanc *17*

ROSÉ WINE
> Blush *21*
> White Zinfandel *23*

RED WINE
> Burgundy *28*
> Merlot *31*
> Petite Sirah *32*
> Pinot Noir *33*
> Zinfandel *34*

Ethnic Foods

French

Creamy foods, lots of sauces, rich, heavy fare; watch the diet.

CHAMPAGNE
Blanc de Blancs *5*
Blanc de Noirs *6*
Brut *7*

WHITE WINE
Chardonnay *12*
Sauvignon Blanc *17*

RED WINE
Cabernet Sauvignon *29*
Gamay Beaujolais *30*
Merlot *31*
Pinot Noir *33*

—— *Notes* ——

Italian

Lots of garlic, oregano, and basil in a tomato sauce, or simply pasta with garlic and spices speaks Italian.

—— *Notes* ——

RED WINE

Barbera *27*
Burgundy *28*
Cabernet Sauvignon *29*
Merlot *31*
Petite Sirah *32*
Zinfandel *34*

Oriental

Stir fry vegetables with a dash of soy served with rice and you'll think you're in the Far East.

CHAMPAGNE
Blanc de Blancs *5*
Blanc de Noirs *6*
Extra Dry *8*

WHITE WINE
Chablis *11*
Chardonnay *12*
Chenin Blanc *13*
Gerwürztraminer *14*
Riesling *15*
Sake *16*
Sauvignon Blanc *17*

ROSÉ WINE
Vin Rosé *22*
White Zinfandel *23*

DESSERT WINE
Muscato *37*
Sherry *39*

—— *Notes* ——

Fruits

Fleshy
Melons
Berries

Sweet fruits and melons are great with wine! Tart fruits, such as raspberries, can be served with wine if you have sweetened them with sugar, sweet creams or are served with chocolate. Since almost all melons are sweet, they pair with wine to make a wonderful dessert course.

Fleshy

Apples, Peaches, Pears

—— *Notes* ——

CHAMPAGNE
Blanc de Blancs *5*
Blanc de Noirs *6*
Brut *7*
Extra Dry *8*

WHITE WINE
Chablis *11*
Chardonnay *12*
Chenin Blanc *13*
Gerwürztraminer *14*
Riesling *15*

ROSÉ WINE
Blush *21*
Vin Rosé *22*
White Zinfandel *23*

RED WINE
Gamay Beaujolais *30*
Pinot Noir *33*

DESSERT WINE
Muscato *37*
Port *38*

Fruits

Melons

Cantaloupe, Honey Dew, Casaba

—— *Notes* ——

CHAMPAGNE
Blanc de Blancs *5*
Blanc de Noirs *6*
Brut *7*
Extra Dry *8*

WHITE WINE
Chablis *11*
Chardonnay *12*
Chenin Blanc *13*
Gerwürztraminer *14*
Riesling *15*

ROSÉ WINE
Blush *21*
Vin Rosé *22*
White Zinfandel *23*

RED WINE
Gamay Beaujolais *30*
Pinot Noir *33*

DESSERT WINE
Muscato *37*

Fruits

Berries

Raspberries, Strawberries, Grapes

—— *Notes* ——

CHAMPAGNE
Blanc de Blancs *5*
Blanc de Noirs *6*
Brut *7*
Extra Dry *8*

WHITE WINE
Chablis *11*
Chardonnay *12*
Chenin Blanc *13*
Gerwürztraminer *14*
Riesling *15*
Sauvignon Blanc *17*

ROSÉ WINE
Blush *21*
Vin Rosé *22*
White Zinfandel *23*

RED WINE
Gamay Beaujolais *30*
Pinot Noir *33*

DESSERT WINE
Muscato *37*
Port *38*

Fruits

Meats

Beef
Cured
Lamb
Pork
Veal

These wine suggestions may vary from the old rules: "red meat - red wine"; "white meat - white wine." Hard to beat a rack of lamb served with a rich Chardonnay. Since there are no "rules," you are the best judge.

Hint: Marinades and sauces can influence your wine selection.

Beef

—— *notes* ——

ROSÉ WINE
Blush *21*

RED WINE
Barbera *27*
Burgundy *28*
Cabernet Sauvignon *29*
Merlot *31*
Petite Sirah *32*
Pinot Noir *33*
Zinfandel *34*

Meats

Cured

Ham, Salami, Prosciutto

CHAMPAGNE
Blanc de Noirs *6*
Brut *7*
Extra Dry *8*

WHITE WINE
Chenin Blanc *13*
Gerwürztraminer *14*
Riesling *15*
Sauvignon Blanc *17*

ROSÉ WINE
Blush *21*
White Zinfandel *23*

RED WINE
Barbera *27*
Burgundy *28*
Gamay Beaujolais *30*
Merlot *31*
Petite Sirah *32*
Pinot Noir *33*
Zinfandel *34*

DESSERT WINE
Port *38*

—— *Notes* ——

Meats

Lamb

Meats

Pork

Also See Cured Meats

Also See Cured Meats

CHAMPAGNE
Blanc de Blancs *5*
Blanc de Noirs *6*
Brut *7*
Extra Dry *8*

WHITE WINE
Chablis *11*
Chardonnay *12*
Chenin Blanc *13*
Gerwürztraminer *14*
Riesling *15*
Sauvignon Blanc *17*

ROSÉ WINE
Blush *21*
White Zinfandel *23*

RED WINE
Burgundy *28*
Gamay Beaujolais *30*
Merlot *31*
Pinot Noir *33*

notes

Meats

72

Veal

—— *Notes* ——

CHAMPAGNE
Blanc de Blancs *5*
Blanc de Noirs *6*
Brut *7*
Extra Dry *8*

WHITE WINE
Chablis *11*
Chardonnay *12*
Chenin Blanc *13*
Gerwürztraminer *14*
Riesling *15*
Sauvignon Blanc *17*

ROSÉ WINE
Blush *21*
White Zinfandel *23*

RED WINE
Burgundy *28*
Gamay Beaujolais *30*
Pinot Noir *33*

Poultry

Light
Dark

The cooking methods, ranging from sautéing, frying, or barbecuing, can influence your wine choices.

Hint: Use a lighter wine with a lighter cooking method.

Light

Lighter Flavored Fowl;
Chicken, Turkey, Cornish Game Hens

—— *Notes* ——

CHAMPAGNE
Blanc de Blancs *5*
Blanc de Noirs *6*
Brut *7*
Extra Dry *8*

WHITE WINE
Chablis *11*
Chardonnay *12*
Chenin Blanc *13*
Gerwürztraminer *14*
Sauvignon Blanc *17*

ROSÉ WINE
Vin Rosé *22*
White Zinfandel *23*

RED WINE
Pinot Noir *33*

Poultry

Dark

Stronger Flavored Fowl;
Duck, Goose, Quail

CHAMPAGNE
Brut *7*

ROSÉ WINE
Blush *21*

RED WINE
Barbera *27*
Burgundy *28*
Cabernet Sauvignon *29*
Gamay Beaujolais *30*
Merlot *31*
Petite Sirah *32*
Pinot Noir *33*
Zinfandel *34*

—— *Notes* ——

Salads

(Green, Pasta, or Rice)

Vinegar or Lemon Dressing
Creamy Dressing

Because of the high vinegar content in salad dressings, I use a great deal of discretion in serving wine with a simple green salad - try Rosé. Add shrimp to the salad, chill a bottle of Gerwürztraminer, break french bread and enjoy!

Vinegar or Lemon Dressings

Italian, Caesar

—— *Notes* ——

CHAMPAGNE
Blanc de Blancs *5*
Blanc de Noirs *6*
Brut *7*
Extra Dry *8*

WHITE WINE
Chenin Blanc *13*
Gerwürztraminer *14*
Riesling *15*
Sauvignon Blanc *17*

ROSÉ WINE
Blush *21*
Vin Rosé *22*
White Zinfandel *23*

RED WINE
Gamay Beaujolais *30*

Salads

Creamy Dressings

Ranch, Thousand Island, French

CHAMPAGNE
Blanc de Blancs *5*
Brut *7*

WHITE WINE
Chablis *11*
Chardonnay *12*
Chenin Blanc *13*
Gerwürztraminer *14*
Riesling *15*
Sauvignon Blanc *17*

ROSÉ WINE
Blush *21*
Vin Rosé *22*
White Zinfandel *23*

RED WINE
Gamay Beaujolais *30*
Zinfandel *34*

—— *Notes* ——

Salads

Sauces

Creamy
Gravies-Meat Stocks
Tomato

These pairings, like the soup pairings, are fairly straightforward. The major "wild card" is the strength of the spice (i.e., curry). When in doubt, find the item with which the sauce is to be served and use that choice. If the dish is very complex, pick the dominant flavor and serve a complementary wine.

Creamy

CHAMPAGNE
Blanc de Blancs *5*
Blanc de Noirs *6*
Brut *7*
Extra Dry *8*

WHITE WINE
Chablis *11*
Chardonnay *12*
Chenin Blanc *13*
Gerwürztraminer *14*
Riesling *15*
Sauvignon Blanc *17*

ROSÉ WINE
Vin Rosé *22*
White Zinfandel *23*

DESSERT WINE
Sherry *39*

Sauces

Gravies - Meat Stocks

CHAMPAGNE
Brut *7*

—— *notes* ——

WHITE WINE
Gerwürztraminer *14*
Riesling *15*

RED WINE
Barbera *27*
Burgundy *28*
Cabernet Sauvignon *29*
Merlot *31*
Petite Sirah *32*
Pinot Noir *33*
Zinfandel *34*

Sauces

Tomato

ROSÉ WINE
Blush *21*

RED WINE
Barbera *27*
Burgundy *28*
Cabernet Sauvignon *29*
Merlot *31*
Petite Sirah *32*
Zinfandel *34*

Sauces

Sausages

Light
Dark

The many regional differences in spices and styles make sausages a natural candidate for experimentation. Try a "Cincinnati chili dog" and a glass of Merlot or an upstate New York "brat" and a glass of Blanc de Blancs.

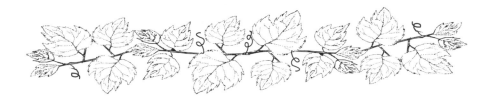

Light

Lighter Flavored;
Chicken, Turkey, Veal

—— *notes* ——

CHAMPAGNE
Blanc de Blancs *5*
Blanc de Noirs *6*
Brut *7*
Extra Dry *8*

WHITE WINE
Chablis *11*
Chardonnay *12*
Chenin Blanc *13*
Gerwürztraminer *14*
Riesling *15*
Sauvignon Blanc *17*

ROSÉ WINE
Vin Rosé *22*
White Zinfandel *23*

RED WINE
Burgundy *28*
Gamay Beaujolais *30*
Pinot Noir *33*

Sausages

91

Dark

Stronger Flavored;
Beef, Venison and other Wild Game

ROSÉ WINE
Blush *21*
White Zinfandel *23*

RED WINE
Barbera *27*
Burgundy *28*
Cabernet Sauvignon *29*
Gamay Beaujolais *30*
Merlot *31*
Petite Sirah *32*
Pinot Noir *33*
Zinfandel *34*

—— *Notes* ——

Seafood

Fish
Shellfish

Fresh fish prepared in almost any fashion
goes well with wine. The stronger flavored,
(i.e., salmon) need a "bigger bodied" wine.

Fish

Cod, Sole, Red Snapper

CHAMPAGNE
 Blanc de Blancs *5*
 Brut *7*
 Extra Dry *8*

WHITE WINE
 Chablis *11*
 Chardonnay *12*
 Chenin Blanc *13*
 Gerwürztraminer *14*
 Riesling *15*
 Sauvignon Blanc *17*

ROSÉ WINE
 Vin Rosé *22*
 White Zinfandel *23*

Seafood

Shellfish

Clams, Crab, Shrimp

CHAMPAGNE
Blanc de Blancs *5*
Blanc de Noirs *6*
Brut *7*
Extra Dry *8*

WHITE WINE
Chablis *11*
Chardonnay *12*
Chenin Blanc *13*
Gerwürztraminer *14*
Riesling *15*
Sauvignon Blanc *17*

ROSÉ WINE
Blush *21*
Vin Rosé *22*
White Zinfandel *23*

RED WINE
Gamay Beaujolais *30*
Pinot Noir *33*

DESSERT WINE
Sherry *39*

—— *Notes* ——

Soups

Creamy
Light
Hearty

When I am making my personal wine choice, I simply use the same guidelines that I have for sauces. The wine pairing for sauces and soups are usually interchangeable.

Creamy

—— *Notes* ——

CHAMPAGNE
  Blanc de Blancs *5*
  Blanc de Noirs *6*
  Brut *7*
  Extra Dry *8*

WHITE WINE
  Chablis *11*
  Chardonnay *12*
  Chenin Blanc *13*
  Sauvignon Blanc *17*

ROSÉ WINE
  Vin Rosé *22*
  White Zinfandel *23*

DESSERT WINE
  Sherry *39*

Light

CHAMPAGNE
   Blanc de Blancs *5*
   Brut *7*
   Extra Dry *8*

WHITE WINE
   Chablis *11*
   Chardonnay *12*
   Chenin Blanc *13*
   Sauvignon Blanc *17*

—— *notes* ——

Hearty

——— notes ———

ROSÉ WINE
　Blush *21*

RED WINE
　Barbera *27*
　Burgundy *28*
　Cabernet Sauvignon *29*
　Gamay Beaujolais *30*
　Merlot *31*
　Petite Sirah *32*
　Pinot Noir *33*
　Zinfandel *34*

DESSERT WINE
　Port *38*

Soups

Vegetables

Leafy
Root and Pod

With the exception of a complete vegetarian meal, and since vegetables are generally not served alone, my wine choice is dependent upon the entree. The exception is: If everything else is bland and the vegetable (turnip, squash, etc.) is the predominant flavor, choose from the following list.

Leafy

Spinach, Chard, Greens

—— *Notes* ——

CHAMPAGNE
Blanc de Blancs *5*
Brut *7*

WHITE WINE
Chablis *11*
Chardonnay *12*
Chenin Blanc *13*
Sauvignon Blanc *17*

ROSÉ WINE
Vin Rosé *22*
White Zinfandel *23*

Vegetables

Root and Pod

Carrots, Corn, Peas, Squashes

CHAMPAGNE
    Blanc de Blancs *5*
    Blanc de Noirs *6*
    Brut *7*
    Extra Dry *8*

WHITE WINE
    Chardonnay *12*
    Riesling *15*
    Sauvignon Blanc *17*

ROSÉ WINE
    Blush *21*

RED WINE
    Burgundy *28*
    Gamay Beaujolais *30*
    Zinfandel *34*

—— *Notes* ——

MENUS

Holiday and Seasonal
Ethnic, Regional, and Vegetarian
Summertime Fun
Pairing Party

Complete with Wine Choices
and Selected Recipes

A feast of things, a feast of wine . . .

The Bible, Isaiah 25.6

Holiday and Seasonal Menus

New Year's Day Dinner
Valentine's Day Treats
St. Patrick's Day Dinner
Easter Dinner
Mother's Day Brunch
Memorial Day Barbecue
Father's Day Dinner
Fourth of July Picnic
Vacation Camp
Labor Day Barbecue
Fall Feast
Thanksgiving Dinner
Christmas Dinner

New Year's Day

These are great nibblers (especially fun with champagne) to enjoy while taking down the Christmas tree or watching the football games.

Appetizers*
Chips & Dips
Cheese Platter
Various Sausages
Fruits

 Blanc de Noirs *6*
White Zinfandel *23*

*Appetizers

Slice Brie into 3/8" layers using dental floss
Layer Brie and smoked salmon slices**
Cover top and bottom with fresh dill
Chill overnight
Slice into wedges and garnish with caviar if desired

***Salmon substitutes: fresh fruits, nuts, dried fruits, etc.*

Slice buffalo mozzarella cheese into rounds about the size of the sun-dried sliced tomato in olive oil
Thinly slice red onion
Gently toss:
    cheese
    tomato (with its oil)
    onion rings
    a dash of rice wine vinegar
Marinate for about 2 hours
Remove from marinade; add salt and pepper
Interweave tomato with cheese rounds on a bed of lettuce leaves; top with onion rings

Valentine's Day

With all the fruit in this recipe, you can serve this dish in the morning and still call it "good for you" food. What a way to wake up your sweetheart on Valentine's Day!

Candy
Chocolate Fondue*
Desserts

 Extra Dry Champagne *8*
Cabernet Sauvignon *29*

*Chocolate Fondue

Mix in fondue pot until melted:
    6 oz. bag of semisweet chocolate chips
    1 can sweetened condensed evaporated milk
    Dash of cinnamon
    1/2 tsp. vanilla

Serve warm with:
sliced bananas
fresh strawberries
mandarin oranges
pineapple cubes

St. Patrick's Day

No one makes better corned beef and cabbage than my little Irish mother-in-law, Millie. Following are some of her favorite recipes I *"borrowed."*

*Apple Walnut Salad**
*Corned Beef**
Boiled Potatoes
Carrots
Cabbage
Onions
Biscuits
Boston Cream Pie

 Extra Dry Champagne *8*
Gerwürztraminer *14*

*Apple Walnut Salad

Core and dice 2 red and 2 green apples
Toss with 1 tablespoon lemon juice
Add:
   1/2 cup chopped celery
   1/4 cup chopped walnuts
   1/4 cup raisins
Blend:
   1/4 cup mayonnaise
   1/4 cup sour cream
   1 tbsp. sugar
Gently toss and chill
Lightly sprinkle allspice on top and serve cold
Serves 6

*Corned Beef

Place corned beef with seasoning packet or pickling spices in cold water to cover. Add 1 cup white wine (whatever is available), and bring to a boil. Reduce heat and simmer, cooking until tender, 3 to 5 hours. Remove approximately 1/2 hour before done.
Add:
   6 medium potatoes
   3 carrots, quartered
   1 large onion spiked with 6 cloves
While corned beef is resting, cook the vegetables in the remaining broth (you may need to add more water or wine to cover). Cook covered, on low heat, for 10 minutes:
Add:
   The corned beef
   1 cabbage cut into wedges
   Cover and cook for 20 minutes

Easter

Easter lilies and spring blossoms; winter's done; sunshine is on the way. This menu can be easily taken to the park for your family outing.

Ambrosia Salad *
Glazed Ham *
Baked Yams
Fresh Peas
Dinner Rolls
Lemon Cake

 Blanc de Noirs *6*
Chenin Blanc *13*

*Ambrosia Salad

Dice assorted seasonal fruits and melons (canned fruit can be substituted) to equal 2 cups; set aside and drain juice for ham glaze
Combine:
  1 cup whipped topping and
  1/4 tsp. Spearmint flavoring
Toss gently and chill
Serve cold with mint leaf or cherry garnish

*Glaze for Ham

Heat together:
  1/4 cup white wine
  juice from the fruit above
  horseradish mustard to taste
Begin basting every 20 minutes after ham is approximately half cooked

Mother's Day Brunch

This is my wife's favorite because the kids do the work
and there's no mess (well, maybe a little)!

Strawberry Waffles*
Whipped Cream
Canadian Bacon

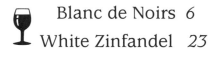 Blanc de Noirs 6
White Zinfandel *23*

*Strawberry Waffles

In a bowl, thaw 1 pint frozen sliced strawberries
Heat frozen waffles following package directions
Place 1 - 2 tablespoons strawberries on waffle
Top with whipped cream or sprinkle with powered sugar
Serve with love

Memorial Day

My brother always barbecues the chicken. That's why
the sauce is so important. Some are
less likely to char than others.

Barbecued Chicken*
Potato Salad
Corn on the Cob
French Bread
Apple Pie

 White Zinfandel *23*

Zinfandel *34*

*Barbecue Sauce

Mix:
    1 cup oil
    1/2 cup vinegar
    1/2 cup white wine
Add:
    1 tbsp. Italian seasoning
    1 tsp. minced garlic
    1/2 tsp. onion powder
    salt and pepper to taste

Reserve 1/2 cup of marinade. Marinate chicken in remainder
for 2 hours, then discard marinade
Mix reserved marinade with 1/4 cup catsup and baste the
chicken the last 15 minutes of cooking

Father's Day

This day is for me, but I'm still the chef.
How does that work?

Spinach Salad*
New York Steak
Cottage Fries
Peas and Onions
Cake

 Merlot *31*
Petite Sirah *32*

* Spinach Salad

Dressing:
Mix and chill:
    1/4 cup olive oil
    1/4 cup wine vinegar
    1 tbsp. lemon juice
    1 tbsp. sugar
    1/2 tsp. salt

Salad:
Wash 1 bunch spinach leaves thoroughly
Slice 2 hard-boiled eggs
Thinly slice 1 small red onion
Fry 4 slices diced bacon until crisp, and dry on
    paper towel; cool
Toss salad ingredients with chilled dressing
Top with cracked black pepper

Fourth of July

Another family favorite! Food and wine taste just as good on paper plates and in paper cups as they do on china and in crystal.

Hamburgers & Hot Dogs
Baked Beans*
Chips
Carrots
Stuffed Celery
Olives
Watermelon

 Blanc de Noirs *6*
White Zinfandel *23*

*Lisa's "Firecracker" Baked Beans

An apt description of my daughter Lisa's personality…

    Open a can of baked beans
    Place in casserole dish
    Chop equal amounts:
       onions
       fresh hot chili peppers
    Mix well and bake at 325° for 45 minutes
    Serve warm

August

You can make the jardiniere as spicy hot as you like
by adding fresh whole hot peppers. It's fun to make at home
with the family in anticipation of your vacation.
Also great as a snack food.

Vacation - Camp Menu
Jardiniere*
Wood-roasted Choice of Meat
Campfire-Baked Potato
Corn on the Cob
Fresh Fruit

 Chablis *11*
Burgundy *28*

*Jardiniere

Empty a jar of pepperoncini with juice into a plastic
container with tight-fitting lid
Add fresh chunks of cauliflower, carrots, celery and onions
Finish filling jar with distilled water
Tightly close lid and place in cool spot overnight
or up to 3 months
Serve cold

Labor Day

This day of rest (why is it called *Labor* Day?) signals the end of summer. School is starting, families are returning to routines and those without children are making vacation plans. This meal should be easy and fun, so if you want, buy prepared foods and add your personal touch.

Barbecued Ribs*
Macaroni Salad
Ranch Beans
Cake

 Merlot *31*
Pinot Noir *33*

*Barbecue Sauce

Sauté chopped onions and minced garlic in equal portions of oil and Worcestershire sauce
Add catsup, brown sugar, mustard, and a splash of orange juice
Or purchase your favorite sauce
Season to taste with salt, black pepper, and choice of hot sauce, diced jalapeños or cayenne pepper
Baste often

Fall Feast

There is nothing better than "comfort" foods when the weather starts to change and the leaves begin to fall.

Cream Soup*
Roast Pork
Scalloped Potatoes
Corn
Apple Sauce
Corn Bread
Pumpkin Cookies

 Chenin Blanc *13*

Mulled Wine

*Cream Soup

Peel and chop yellow squash to equal 1 cup (other root vegetables can be substituted)

Sauté 1 chopped onion in butter

To onions, add 2 cups chicken broth (can use 2 bouillon cubes with 2 cups water), squash, and bouquet garni (bay leaf, parsley stalk, marjoram and thyme sprigs, all tied in cheese cloth)

Cook until tender, remove and discard bouquet garni

Blend mixture in food processor

Serve warm topped with a dollop of sour cream

Thanksgiving

Almost everyone's favorite holiday. Family and friends
get together just to celebrate food and fellowship.

Antipasto
Turkey with Stuffing*
Sweet Potatoes
Mashed Potatoes
Gravy
Mixed Vegetables
Cranberry Sauce
Dinner Rolls*
Favorite Pies

 Blanc de Noirs 6

Pinot Noir 33

*Stuffing for Turkey

(Proportions given are for 12 - 15 lb. turkey)
    Boil turkey neck and giblets with:
        1/2 onion
        celery tops
        poultry seasoning
        salt and pepper
until meat is well cooked
Strain, saving the broth and giblets
Sauté in butter until soft:
    1 cup chopped onions
    2 cups chopped celery
Add:
    12 cups bread cubes
    diced cooked giblets with broth to moisten
Mix by hand just until mixtures bind together. Adjust
seasonings and liquid to your preference (dry or moist)
and stuff bird

This stuffing may also be baked in a separate foil-covered dish
Coat turkey with butter. Bake in 325° preheated oven. Baste with butter every 20 minutes until done (leg moves easily away from the joint), approximately 4 hours

*Bread

Thaw 1 loaf store-bought, frozen bread dough
Slice into 3 equal portions
Roll each piece into a 12" rope
Braid the 3 ropes, form them into a circle, brush with eggwash or butter. Top with sesame seeds and bake according to package directions
Serve warm

Christmas

This is truly a wondrous time. We have watched with glee: the little ones with their gifts and the one who has received that special something. Now let's celebrate this holiday with a wonderful meal.

Tossed Green Salad
Prime Rib
Baked Potato / Sour Cream
Yorkshire Pudding*
Creamed Spinach
Cheesecake

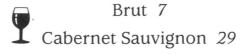

Brut *7*
Cabernet Sauvignon *29*

*Yorkshire Pudding

Mix:
   2 eggs
   1 cup milk
   1 cup flour
Blend until smooth. Do not overbeat (will reduce volume)
Pour in baking dish that has been preheated in 425° oven
Drizzle 1/2 cup beef drippings over batter
Bake approximately 35 minutes and serve warm
Serves 6 to 9

Ethnic, Regional, and Vegetarian Menus

Cajun
French
Italian
Oriental
Seafood
Southwestern
Vegetarian

Cajun

I was surprised to find that a number of people have not tried okra. However, it is the mainstay in chicken gumbo and the vegetable of choice for many Southerners.

Shrimp Cocktail
Lobster Bisque
Blackened Catfish
Red Beans & Rice
Fried Okra*
Fruit Tart

 Riesling *15*
Pinot Noir *33*

*Fried Okra

In a bag mix:
    corn meal
    salt and pepper
Add sliced okra and shake the bag to coat each piece
Fry in hot oil or bacon fat until golden brown and crisp
Drain on paper plate and serve warm

French

No one appreciates wine with food like the French,
who often enjoy two-hour meals featuring a different
wine with each course.

Duck Confit Salad
Stuffed Artichoke Hearts*
Rack of Lamb
Wild Mushroom Medley
White Beans with Sun-dried Tomatoes
Fruit and Cheese

Brut 7
Pinot Noir *33*

*Stuffed Artichoke Hearts

Wash 6 artichokes and place in lightly salted boiling water
Cook until leaves pull out easily; drain and chill
Remove all leaves and "choke," leaving only the cap
Reserve the caps and finely dice the artichoke hearts
Sauté 1 1/2 cups sliced mushrooms in:
    1/4 cup sherry
    3/4 cup water
    1 packet chicken gravy mix
Carefully fold in:
    the diced hearts
    1 cup shredded Swiss cheese
    a pinch each of marjoram and thyme
    salt and pepper
Stuff the caps with this mixture and lightly sprinkle bread
crumbs on top
Broil until brown and serve warm

Italian

Italian cooks seem to be able to take a clove of garlic and a tomato and turn it into a four-course meal. Serve the meal with a hearty red wine.

Antipasto
Green Salad
Tortellini with Sun-dried Tomatoes*
Sauteed Zucchini
Spumoni Ice Cream

 Burgundy *28*
Zinfandel *34*

*Tortellini with Sun-dried Tomatoes

Cook tortellini per package instructions
Gently sauté (or microwave) until soft:
    1 cup rough-chopped sun-dried tomatoes with their oil
    1 tbsp. minced garlic
Toss tortellini, tomato mix, basil, salt and pepper
Top with fresh Parmesan

Oriental

This fried rice recipe is not as difficult as it appears, but if you've had a long day, use a box mix or steamed rice for this meal. Fruity, slightly sweet wines are best.

Won Ton Soup
Egg Rolls
Cashew Chicken
Sweet & Sour Pork
Chow Mein
Barbecued Pork-Fried Rice*
Fortune Cookie

Blanc de Noirs *6*
Chenin Blanc *13*
Sake *16*

*Barbecued Pork-Fried Rice

Cook 2 cups raw rice (adding 1 tablespoon oil) per package instructions and then chill well
Beat and fry 2 eggs as a thin pancake
Dice 1/2 cup cooked pork or ham and warm in barbecue sauce
Thinly slice 4 green onions and eggs
Heat wok or large skillet with 1 tablespoon cooking oil and 2 teaspoons sesame seed oil
Stir-fry rice in 3 tablespoons soy sauce until well coated
Add diced green onions, diced eggs, frozen peas and cooked meat. Heat thoroughly. Add soy sauce if necessary
Serve warm with sliced green onions as garnish

Seafood

This is a great dinner for all seasons. It is also one of my
mother, Faye's, favorites during a cold winter rain.
A buttery Chardonnay truly enhances this meal.

Clam Chowder *
Cole Slaw
Grilled Sole
Steamed Potatoes
Baby Lima Beans
Sherbet

 Blanc de Blancs *5*

Chardonnay *12*

*Clam Chowder

Fry 1/4 pound diced bacon until crisp; remove bacon
Sauté 1/2 cup diced onion and 1/4 cup diced celery in
bacon grease
In large pot combine:
    cooked bacon
    onions
    celery
    1 bottle of clam juice
    3 cups half and half
    2 cups finely diced potatoes
Cook until potatoes are tender
Add:
    canned clams with juice
    dash of lemon juice
    salt, white pepper, and cayenne pepper if desired
Heat until clams are warm
Serve hot

Southwestern

Fruity, slightly sweet wines make this summertime early evening dinner a delight. Try barbecueing the chicken!

Guacamole Salad*
Chicken Fajitas
Fruit Salsa
Black Beans
Rice
Sorbet

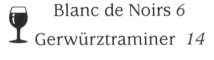 Blanc de Noirs *6*
Gerwürztraminer *14*

*Guacamole Salad

Mash 2 avocados with 1 tablespoon lemon or lime juice
Fold in:
   1 chopped hard-boiled egg
   1 tsp. minced garlic
   1 tsp. onion
Add:
   salt, chili powder and coriander to taste
Serve on shredded lettuce with fresh diced tomato
as garnish
Lightly sprinkle salad with lemon or lime juice to
prevent discoloring

Vegetarian

My grandson, L.J., likes to make Three-Bean Salad with
a twist – he adds cooked corkscrew noodles.

Marinated Three-Bean Salad*
Grilled Eggplant, Squash & Mushrooms*
Brown Rice
Sherbet or Sorbet

 Brut *7*

Chenin Blanc *13*

*Three-Bean Salad

In a large bowl, combine:
   1 can drained garbanzo beans
   1 can drained string beans
   1 can dark kidney beans in their own juice
Add:
   1/4 cup chopped green and red onion
Combine and add to bowl:
   2 parts red wine vinegar
   1 part olive oil
Season with garlic powder, Parmesan cheese, pinch of
basil, salt and pepper to taste
Chill well and serve cold

*Grilled Vegetables

Slice vegetables:
   yams and potatoes 1/2 inch thick
   squash and eggplant lengthwise
   mushrooms and tomatoes in half

Season vegetables with:
  garlic powder
  olive oil
  salt and pepper to taste
Barbecue until tender
(oven baking in cast iron skillet will also work; bake
at 375° for about 20 minutes turning once)

Summertime
Fun Menus

Picnic 1
Picnic 2
Picnic 3

*My idea of a picnic is to relax. So, depending on
my mood, I may prepare the foods or just buy
everything. Most importantly, I need to find
that "perfect" shade tree.*

Picnic 1

Potato Salad
Olives and Pickles
Choice of Fun Sandwich*
Watermelon
Brownies

 Blanc de Noirs 6
White Zinfandel *23*

*Fun Sandwiches

Sliced avocado, tomato, red onion, and olives
Deli meats and cheeses with Italian dressing
Corned beef topped with coleslaw

139

Picnic 2

Pasta Salad*
Pepper Jack Cheese
Cheddar Cheese
Sliced Turkey Breast
Hard Salami
French Bread
Fresh Apples and Pears

 Extra Dry Champagne *8*

Chardonnay *12*

*Pasta Salad

Cooked assorted colored pasta twists
Add chopped:
    onion
    celery
    green pepper
    hard boiled egg
Add cubed:
    cucumbers
    cheese
    carrots
Toss with:
    Italian dressing
    salt and pepper
    Sprinkle Parmesan cheese on top

Picnic 3

Baby Greens Salad
Quiche*
Fresh Melons

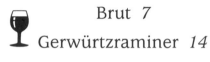

Brut *7*

Gerwürtzraminer *14*

*Quiche

   1 pastry shell, uncooked
   Chopped spinach (one bunch fresh or one box frozen)
   3 strips bacon, cooked and crumbled
   Chopped onion sauteed in bacon grease; drained
   Mix together:
      3 eggs
      1/2 cup milk
      1/2 cup heavy cream
   Add:
      Spinach, bacon and cooked onion
   Pour into pie shell and bake in preheated oven 375°
   25 minutes or until knife plunged into custard comes
   out clean
   6 servings

Wine and Food Pairings

Let's have a tasting party!

This can be for 1 to 100 people, so choose an idea or two from this list and let's get started. Sip the wine, taste the food, finish with the wine. Trust your taste buds. If this is a good pairing, it will please your palate. Critique it if you wish, using this book to record your notes, or just enjoy the experience. Remember, simplicity and fun are the keynotes to success, and you are the ultimate judge. There are no absolute right or wrong results.

A few ideas.
Try some of your own or
"mix and match."
Your wine, your food, your rules!

Apple pie with Extra Dry Champagne
Caviar with Brut
Chips and dips with Chablis or Burgundy
Cocktail meatballs with Petite Sirah
Dark chocolate with Cabernet Sauvignon
Milk chocolate with Port
Deli meats with Merlot
Egg rolls with Sake
Fruits and cheeses with Chenin Blanc or Blush
Green salad with Riesling
Melons with Brut
Nachos with White Zinfandel
Nuts (all types) with any Sparkling Wine or Champagne
Olives with Sherry
Onion rings with Vin Rosé
Pates with Blanc de Noirs
Pizza with Barbera
Popcorn with Blanc de Blancs
Potato or Macaroni salad with Sauvignon Blanc
Quiche with Chardonnay
Sausages with Gamay Beaujolais
Shrimp or Crab cocktail with Gerwürtztraminer
Smoked salmon with Pinot Noir
Teacakes with Muscato
Vegetables (raw or Cooked) with Zinfandel

Wine Reflections

Food Reflections

Menu Reflections